Book title: "My 30 something nature poems"

Written by: Abiygayil Chephtsiybah Yisrael

2018 copy right My 30 something nature poems by Abiygayil Chephtsiybah Yisrael

All rights reserved.

<u>Acknowledgment:</u>

Thank you God Yahwa, Love-himself, for blessing me with the opportunity to be able to present something nice and refresh for all minds, hearts; also souls. Again, thanks for blessing my mind to be able to think, my fingers to write; also, with the creativity to bring such skill forth with love, joy and laughter.

<u>Dedication:</u>

I dedicated this book of mine to my heavenly

Father Love, my God first, and then to the world.

<u>Recommendation:</u>

I highly recommend this book here to all sorts

of minds; also to all walks of life as well.

Table of contents:

Acknowledgment

Dedication

Recommendation

18. **From up and not of the ground**

19. **When nature is indecisive**

20. **Life**

21. **The heat is at a delay**

22. **It's ah miracle**

23. **A quiet scene**

24. **A burst of life's gratification**

25. **The sun's rays**

26. **The circle of life**

27. **Strange**

28. **Meditation**

29. **In the wild**

30. **Wow the clouds**

31. **It's pollinating**

32. **One silent night**

33. **Hunting season**

34. **Green tea**

35. **Out in the field**

36. **Went fishing**

37. **It's real breezy**

38. **It's windy**

39. **A chilly day**

<u>'It's nature'</u>

It's clear. It's all out there

dropping; dripping

heavily from up here.

Written by: Abiygayil C. Yisrael/ Rhymin Pearl

© **6 hours ago, nature-rhyme • haiku**

Likes: Manche, StoneCausedWaves

StoneCausedWaves - Great work Rhymin Pearl.

Rhymin Pearl - Thanks a lot my dear.

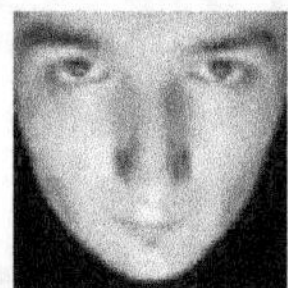

**Manche - Everything that needed to be said its
Written in few lines. Nicely penned,
Thank you for sharing.**

Rhymin Pearl - Thank you very much.

'Keep pollinating'

Bumblebee, I SEE...

THREE of you and now they are FREEZE.

FREE...FREE to buzz around the TREE.

Written by: Abiygayil C. Yisrael/ Rhymin Pearl

© 24 hours ago, nature- • rhyme • Haiku

Likes everyone1

everyone1 - This is glorious friend, oh, how we need them to continue to do this for us. Well thought out, written, friend. Clever write!

Rhymin Pearl - Thanks ah lot my dear friend.

everyone1 - U bet friend.

'Feel the heat'

**It's bright...round
And HOT...and it stays;
and stands in one SPOT.**

Written by: Abiygayil C. Yisrael/ Rhymin Pearl
© 6 hours ago, Abiygayil C. Yisrael nature-rhyme •
haiku

Likes: Glassrose48, Nimaanmi

**Nimaanmi - The start of the winter, and a
heat saying, nice to feel the heat. ☺**

Rhymin Pearl - How was my poem there?

Nimaanmi - It's really good, I felt the warmth ☺

Rhymin Pearl - Thank you so much.

Nimaanmi - ☺

<u>**'Something to look forward for'**</u>

Something FUNNY.

Look HUNNY. Do you see?

My BUNNY…SUNNY?

Written by: Abiygayil C. Yisrael/ Rhymin Pearl

© 6 days ago,

Likes: Labella amare r., Senthea Diamond

Labella amare r. - Nice laugh.

Rhymin Pearl - Thank you.

Labella amare r. - You are welcome

Senthea Diamond - Love it very different Hunny, Bunny twist it was definitely funny!

'Fish in a clear pond'

Looking though a crystal bowl,
water to my knees, I saw a big one,
right before I left.

Written by: Abiygayil C.Yisrael/ Rhymin Pearl
© 10 months ago, nature • haiku

Likes pentopaper41

pentopaper41 - I can see the clear water.
I can see the big fish swim by my feet. Lovely!

Rhymin Pearl - Thanks so much.

'God has caused'

The Sun to rise.

Oh, what ah DELIGHT

God didn't shorten us

His glorious LIGHT.

He always knows

How to make our day

so BRIGHT and quite ALRIGHT.

And if it's like that...I can't

Wait for TONIGHT.

Written by: Abiygayil C. Yisrael/ Rhymin Pearl

© 8 hours ago, nature • rhyme • spiritual

Likes Yukon78

Yukon78 - Short and sweet, straight to the point. Moreover, without the love of God we wouldn't be able to enjoy the things he do.

Rhymin Pearl - Thanks ah lot my dear; for commenting and for stopping by.

'In the jungle'

Skin black as coal

Eyes green as grass

Teeth white as snow

And claws sharp as razor

And it pounce on its prey

Its muscle s of its jaw and FANGS

BANGS and deeply penetrates its

prey flesh. WRESTLE and TUSSLE

while jaw shut TIGHT with all its MIGHT

until the prey is lifeless isn't

It ah mess until it's over phew!

No more stress! Now, it's time

to chow down and get much

rest; now I'm at my best. Belly

full claws in and that's the end.

Written by: Abiygayil C. Yisrael/ Rhymin Pearl

© a day ago, nature-rhyme • haiku

Likes: StoneCausedWaves, McLovincraft

McLovincraft - Wow! This is amazing! Your rhyming is great and it's well written. Is it about a black panther?

Keep going!

Rhymin Pearl - Oh and thank you.

McLovincraft - You are welcome, my friend. ☺.

Rhymin Pearl - Yep! U r so right...Lol.☺.

StoneCausedWaves - Amazing! So powerfullywritten Rhymin Pearl.

Rhymin Pearl - Thank you Hun.

'The sweet breeze of love'

You people of heaven

are so SWEET the breeze

you all are blowing. I'm

Feeling it, through my SHEET.

And it feels better than a fan;

Or AC...you see. Great

job loves from ABOVE.

You guys are such ah DOVE

like folks. I love you all.

Written by: Abiygayil C. Yisrael/ Rhymin Pearl

© a day ago,   rhyme • nature • love • spiritual • heavenly

Likes: Coryjb, Freakshow19

Coryjb - Beautiful write, I love the whole thing. Each line is comforting to read.

Rhymin Pearl - Thank you so much.

'The whistling and the tingling the wind'

The whistling of the wind

Running on the skin

And through the hair

You'd never bow out

Of the coolness;

the freshness of

the wind running on

your skin.

As long it keeps

blowing, you're

definitely in...like

the sand on the beach.

Written by: Abiygayil C. Yisrael/ Rhymin Pearl

© 2 days ago, nature • rhyme

Likes: Kenneth Carroll

Kenneth Carroll - Nicely expressed ink splash. Keep Up the good work... Awesome. Good post!

Rhymin Pearl - Thank you so much.

<u>'One out of God's creations'</u>

**Grayish looking spot at NIGHT
and not in the DAYLIGHT.
What is it then?**

Written by: Abiygayil C. Yisrael/ Rhymin Pearl
© 22 days ago, nature-rhyme • haiku

Likes: Fbuser, Brundaban panda

Brundaban panda - Wonderful creation. Poem well illustrates it. Bat is blind at Daylight but has fantastic vision at night.

<u>'The noise'</u>

I hear a LOUD

and rough SOUND

that I don't ALLOW.

Where is it coming from?

Oh, it's behind this DOOR.

Well never, no MORE

that I will put an end to.

Aye, you! Out you go

and no more snoring ALLOW

for you were too LOUD.

Written by: Abiygayil C. Yisrael/ Rhymin Pearl

© 2 days ago, rhyme. nature

Likes iconoclastic

iconoclastic - playful- I got to share it with my sister my brother in law literally sounds like a bear in the night.

Rhymin Pearl - Lol. Thank yah for reading my poem there n 4 commenting.☺.

'It's a Lizard'

Running very loosely

And it WIGGLE; JIGGLE

as it moves. It's rubbery

and jelly looking. It loves

the heat, but it is cold blooded.

Written by: Abiygayil C. Yisrael/ Rhymin Pearl

© 2 days ago, nature-rhyme • haiku

It's hot and wet"

The rain has poured down.

And the steam has risen.

Y? Because the water

has hit the HOT SPOT.

Written by: Abiygayil C. Yisrael/ Rhymin Pearl

© 3 days ago, haiku • nature • rhyme

Likes atkeller44ohio

atkeller44ohio - I think that pretty much answers that. How about the rest of you folks? Nice post!

Rhymin Pearl — Thanks.

atkeller44ohio — No problem.

Likes NickBaker

NickBaker - A pleasing delivery captures the attention nicely and very effectively. Great!

Rhymin Pearl - Thank you so much.

'The existence'

Pull it in

and push it out.

And what do you hear?

God passing and

circling through.

Written by: Abiygayil C. Yisrael/ Rhymin Pearl

© 3 days ago,   rhyme • spiritual • love • hope

Likes Princess adict

**Princess adict - Nice one there. It's brief,
but concise. Keep up the good work. Great!**

'Sunset'

**The sky is gray with
the fiery orange color is
Settling down behind the clouds.**

Written by: Abiygayil C. Yisrael/ Rhymin Pearl

© 3 days ago, nature. rhyme • haiku

Likes: Colin Hughes, Glassrose48

**Colin Hughes - Quite deep really.
Well written poet. Bigger than its mass. Great!**

Rhymin Pearl - Thank very much.

'It's ah blizzard'

It is so bloody cold

Out there, I barely

can move.

Written by: Abiygayil C. Yisrael/Rhymin Pearl

© 3 days ago, haiku nature

Likes Vona Markov

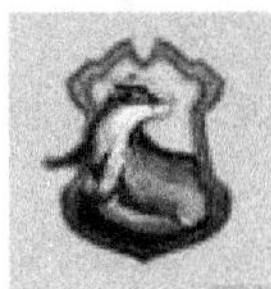

Vona Markov - have you considered writing haikus?
They are great for capturing short thoughts like these.
8/10. Great!

Rhymin Pearl - Thank you so much...I'll consider it.☺.

'Global warning'

It's raining...it's windy

It's sunny and also freezing.

All at once. What could

have gone wrong?

Has all the elements has

gone haywire? Or it is man

tampering with nature?

Written by: Abiygayil C. Yisrael/ Rhymin Pearl

© 3 days ago, nature • -haiku

Likes AndyKalon

AndyKalon - It's humanity's fault. This problem will remain for years. There's constant collision.

Rhymin Pearl - Yeah I know. But how my poem there?

AndyKalon - Your poem has a valid point

Rhymin Pearl - Thanks.

AndyKalon - You're welcome.

'Snow flakes'

Snow flake

Snow flake

Stop falling in the LAKE

And give it ah BREAK.

Before you make a MISTAKE

and bring about an HEARTACHE.

If you don't stop flaking in the LAKE.

Written by : Abiygayil C. Yisrael/ Rhymin Pearl

© a month ago,   rhyme • nature

Likes Liesa01

Liesa01 - I do not know if you meant for this to be lighthearted or not, but that is how I read it. When I read it, it came across as slightly bouncy. It also does seem to allude to human nature as well and mother nature. Loved your poem.

Rhymin Pearl - Thank you.

<u>**'From up and not of the ground'**</u>

It's red

and sweet

and ROUND.

And it's plenty

to go AROUND.

And you can get it

by the POUND.

Written by: Abiygayil C. Yisrael/ Rhymin Pearl

© 3 days ago,   rhyme • nature

Likes Shobha

**Shobha - Nice way to riddle? Is it the Tomato?
Thanks for sharing. Keep writing.**

**Rhymin Pearl - Lol…an apple. Thanks
for reading my poem there.**

<u>'When nature is indecisive'</u>

It changes sometimes,

Sometimes it's WHITE

And sometimes it's dark

I mean black.

Well...better yet!

Sometimes it's

sunny n BRIGHT

and other times,

it's dark like NIGHT.

Written by: Abiygayil C. Yisrael/ Rhymin Pearl

© 3 days ago,   nature • rhyme

Likes: Ralfkay, Jackie Werdlow

**Ralfkay - you write an astute nine-line
poem that makesa strong case for your theme
of Nature's changeability; well-done.**

**Rhymin Pearl - Thanks a lot my dear...I appreciate u 4
reading my poem there; plus 4 stopping by.**

Jackie Werdlow - I like this. The later of the poem
seemedto restate your point. Easy to follow
and cleverly written. Good work.

Rhymin Pearl - Thank you Very much for your
Kind remarks there. I appreciate you
for stopping by; have a great day.

<u>'Life'</u>

Is just ah new

beginning.

Like SPRING

doing its THING.

Written by: Abiygayil C. Yisrael/Rhymin Pearl

© 4 days ago,   rhyme • nature • haiku

Likes: atkeller440ohio, Hearthrob

Hearthrob - Each day new mercies can be found if one is not blinded by sin. Most definitely Concur with your outlook on life. GOD Bless.

atkeller440ohio - You could really say that again, Lady… and nice job on this piece.

Rhymin Pearl - Thanks ah bunch my dear.

atkeller440ohio - My pleasure.

<u>'The heat is at a delay'</u>

The water is cold I guess the sun

has not come out YET. Even though

it's WET. Its heat has not SET.

Written by: Abiygayil C. Yisrael/ Rhymin Pearl

© 14 days ago,   nature-rhyme

<h1 style="text-align:center">Likes Dr.Ram Mehta</h1>

Dr.Ram Mehta - Very nicely penned and crafted piece on the heat of the sun. Liked it.

Rhymin Pearl - Thank you very much my dear.

<u>'It's ah miracle'</u>

Clear skies

birds are FLYING

still alive not DYING.

And nor CRYING.

Feeling good

like I should.

Another day

above the ground

is victorious.

Written by: Abiygayil C. Yisrael/Rhymin Pearl

© **23 days ago,   rhyme • hope • nature • love • happy**

Likes: Fbuser, bornsoltera

**bornsoltera - I like the vibe; so grateful
and content. Keep writing. Brief but says a lot.**

**Rhymin Pearl - Thanks for your comment
there, and for stopping by.**

'A quiet scene'

It's no SOUND AROUND.

I'm chilling...sitting thinking

and staring up in the ATOMSPHERE

Right HERE...but at the same time

My mind is travelling ELSEWHERE

While my body is still HERE; NEAR.

Written by: Abiygayil C. Yisrael/ Rhymin Pearl

© a month ago,　nature-rhyme • spiritual

Likes Cindy B

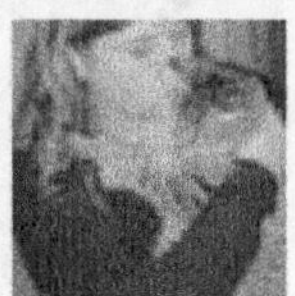

Cindy B - Reading this, I think of a child daydreaming at some favorite, quiet place found by accident on a bike ride...and revisited often. I think of young me.

Rhymin Pearl - Well gee wee...thanks. But how was it though? The poem I mean.

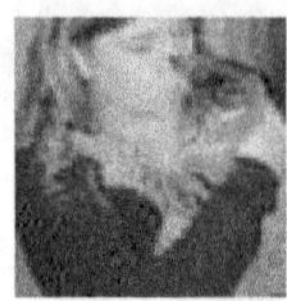

Cindy B - It was wonderful! Any poem that inspires Imagery & feelings in people has done its job.

Rhymin Pearl - Thank you so much.

'A burst of life's gratification'

A rush of sunshine rised early

and a brush of nice; sweet

Breezy attach to it. Has already

started my morning. So Good morning

world; thank God Yahwa- (YHWH)

Yahweh for letting it be.

Written by: Abiygayil C. Yisrael/ Rhymin Pearl

© a day ago, nature • rhyme

Likes Musonda Mulenga

Musonda Mulenga - mm...Try adding coffee to this peace! Why I drink it...all in a cup. Lovely poem indeed...keep going.

Rhymin Pearl - Okay... thank you so much.

'The Sun's ray'

Looking...slipping and PEEPING;

CREEPING through my window

And it is so BRIGHT...high; hot

I can feel the heat in my ROOM.

BOOM...I'm gone out of my room

and I didn't say TOMB...hahaha!

I said room because in ah TOMB I

wouldn't be able to see day LIGHT

at all. Unless being open.

Written by: Abiygayil. C. Yisrael/ Rhymin Pearl

© 2 days ago, rhyme • nature

Likes: Glassrose48, Mariovitale227

Mariovitale227 - Reality very fresh you got here really in its place to come through you know. Nice poem.

Rhymin Pearl - Thank you.

'The circle of life'

Butterflies R all around

me. N I wonder Y?

Y...Y...N.Y.

What do they C

N love about me.

4 I'm not a tree.

U see.

Hee...hee. ..Gee. Wee.

But since I don't know Y...

I'll just have 2 let them be.

4 they R so beautiful

N colorful N most definitely

Quite an interesting flyable little

Creatures. Look how they flow

N that's real slow...N yeah I know.

But Y make the ring around me.

Oh yeah! Now I got it...we R

connected N that's Y they gravitate

towards maw. Haha!

Written by: Abiygayil C. Yisrael/ Rhymin Pearl

© **a day ago, humor • nature-rhyme • spiritual**

Likes Firetrickster

Firetrickster - I really enjoyed the style of this and the free spirit feel to it. Clever work!

Rhymin Pearl - Thank you.

'Strange'

**White clouds with
a ring of darkness.
First time?**

Written by: Abiygayil C. Yisrael/ Rhymin Pearl
© 3 days ago,   nature • haiku

Likes Midnightdream00

Midnightdream00 - Very intriguing poet.

The last line really left me in a nice haze. Keep it up!

Rhymin Pearl - Thanks a lot for

reading my poem n4 stopping by.

'Meditation'

**Listening to no noises
thinking of nothing just
connecting to my inner self.**

Written by: Abiygayil C. Yisrael/ Rhymin Pearl
© 4 days ago, spiritual • nature

Likes: V.Muthu manickam, xorubyy

V.Muthu manickam - Connecting to inner self.

To conquer the rare treasures...truly simple

But factual presentation. Liked it.

Rhymin Pearl - Thank you.

xorubyy - short, simple and sweet ! I have always
Wanted to try meditating and just block out
all thoughts and noise. Great!

Rhymin Pearl - Thanks for commenting so kindly.

<u>In the wild</u>

**You cannot be MILD
or act like a little CHILD.
But in the WILD,
You got to grow up FAST
So you can DASH faster
Than FLASH...because
You got to try to LAST.
If you want to get to the
other level...even if you
got to be a rebel;
I didn't say ah devil.
But you got to know
Many STYLE while you
Are out there...in the WILD.**

Written by: Abiygayil C. Yisrael/ Rhymin Pearl

© 6 days ago, rhyme • nature

Likes Sergio Sanchez

**Sergio Sanchez - A strong piece indeed that's
Meaningful and has a lot to look back on
And decipher thank you. Nicely penned!**

Rhymin Pearl - N u r quite welcome. N thank you too.

Sergio Sanchez - You are welcome.

'Wow the clouds'

**Look at the Vastness
of the CLOUDS.
Wow! I am so PROUD that
they show themselves
among the CROWD; I
thank God Almighty
Yahwa that is ALLOW.
Now can I continue
to follow the CROWD
of the CLOUDS?**

Written by: Abiygayil C. Yisrael/ Rhymin Pearl
© a year ago,   nature • rhyme

Likes Abhiruchi Gadgil

Abhiruchi Gadgil - Beautiful!

- Lovely

Rhymin Pearl - Thank you so much.

'It's pollinating'

It's black n yellow gold

And it buzz all the time

When making its rounds.

And so, watch out it doesn't

sting you from behind.

Written by: Abiygayil C. Yisrael/ Rhymin Pearl

© 5 hours ago, nature

Likes Keith Seaman

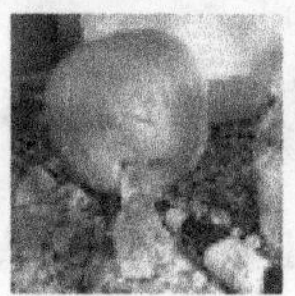

**Keith Seaman - There's that Rhymin Pearl girl! This time
I caught her talking about the birds and the bees!
Lol. Nicely penned.**

**Rhymin Pearl - Thank you commenting and for sharing
Your thoughts there, I appreciate you for stopping by.**

<u>'One silent night'</u>

One silent night

All rats...cats; dogs

Was not active not

Even nature's elements

Was at play I mean practically

Nothing no moves...no sounds

Just pure silence in the NIGHT

It was ALRIGHT to me. It was

Like a peaceful MOMENT

without a TORMENT everything

seemed in place with God's grace.

Written by: Abiygayil C. Yisrael/ Rhymin Pearl

© a day ago, Nature, Life

Likes: Gabiinscore, Syde Affect

Syde Affect - This poem captures the peace found only at night. I like how you compare a peaceful moment to God's grace. As David Byrne once sang, "Heaven is a place where nothing ever happens." You captured the feeling of peace in the night in 10 lines. Just great.

Rhymin Pearl - Thanks a lot. I appreciate You for stopping by.

Gabiinscore - This is a very creative poem! "Without a torment, everything seemed in place" such a powerful words. Nicely done.

Rhymin Pearl - Well, gee…wee…thank so much for commenting so kindly.☺.

'Green tea'

It's hot and green
and sweet; it settles
In ah cup. Watch out
now so it won't drop.

Written by: Reinbowbryte/ Chephtsiybah. Yisrael

© 5 days ago,   haiku • nature-rhyme

Likes Maudzen15

Maudzen15 - Reading this poem tastes so nicely, lovely brevity ☺Great.

Reinbowbryte - Thank you so kindly.

Maudzen15 - My pleasure☺.

<u>'Hunting season'</u>

**Gunshot fired
something fell from the sky
Hit the ground and die.**

Written by: Reinbowbryte/ Chephtsiybah A. Yisrael
© 9 days ago, nature • sad • pain • haiku

Likes GentleSoul

GentleSoul - A true great piece of artwork masterfully well written terrific poem.

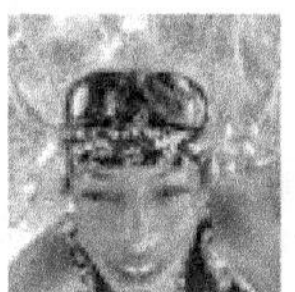

Reinbowbryte - Thank you.

'Out in the field'

Look ah far

what do you see

well ah...I see

the grass...

The weed

and ah what is

that moving towards

my way? Oh my god

It's ah RACOON!

What did you say?

Ah TYCOON? No!

I said ah RACOON.

And so, I best run home.

And be SAFE...but slow

down before I get CHAFE.

Written by: Reinbowbryte/ Chephtsiybah Yisrael

© 9 days ago, rhyme • humor • nature

Likes GentleSoul

GentleSoul - Great piece of masterful artwork truly amazing how well written this is.

'Went fishing'

Look at the fishes

Down below…swimming

Real slow hey here's one

Kind of close; that'll make

A great dish after seasoning.

Written by: Abiygayil C. Yisrael/ Rhymin Pearl

© 4 hours ago, nature • rhyme

Likes: Knuckles

Knuckles - Wow sounds good hope it's catfish (yum) like this one short and sweet a good Read... keep up the good work.

Rhymin Pearl - Well, gee...wee thank you so much my dear; I   appreciate you for stopping by.

<u>'It's real breezy'</u>

Yeah the breeze feels so NICE

It made me to think of ICE.

And I didn't even have

to think TWICE. CHRIST.

© 2 months ago,   rhyme • nature • teen

Likes: Scott Christian, Nassy Fesharaki

Nassy Fesharaki - Abiygayil, short, rich, meaningful, scary and refreshing...Inspired.

Scott Christian - love your rhymes, Pearl!
I live in New Orleans, so any breeze during a southern summer is like a private miracle. Nicely written.

Rhymin Pearl - Yes its breezy in Miami for now...
by the way thanks for your kind comment there.

<u>'It's a windy day'</u>

And the wind is blowing sweetly and softly
SLIDING and GLIDING across my pecan-delighted skin.
I'm enjoying every moment of it BIT by BIT and as long it
doesn't QUIT blowing, I will continue to SIT, and
let it HIT me still, as long as I can stand it. The WIND
REMINDS me of the winter is coming after the storming
of hurricane Matthew has left BEHIND. I am enjoying
this beautiful after math, the wind of course, is
HOWLING; also, BLOWING while it is tickling my SKIN
like a feather being brush up on it. But anyways, with
this KIND of weather here, circling around,
I am relaxing and being refreshed within my MIND, soul
and also spirit; this is the amazing something that I have
been privileged with the gift from the most High
God, King and Father Yahwa.
And so, why even bother to go any farther
When this beautiful WIND is doing
me IN. Like a good FRIEND.

Written by: Abiygayil C. Yisrael/ Rhymin Pearl
© 2 years ago,   nature • rhyme

Likes: Harvey Burklo, Crystal da rock

Crystal da rock - Nice n i enjoyed it. But correct that one typo almost at the end. Thanks for sharing. It must Has been the wind at the end huh Pearl? Lol... Good job! Crystal, a diamond in a rock.

Rhymin Pearl - Lol... thank you for your lovely comments but that typo you are referring to, is exactly what you see there is what I wanted in there. Again thank you and for checking in on my work☺.

Harvey Burklo – Lovely! Enjoy reading keep on writing.

Rhymin Pearl - Thank you very much☺.

'A chilly day'

Woke up to a chilly DAY,

but anyway, what can I SAY

when God made it that WAY.

So, good morning to ALL

while I decide to CRAWL

right back in my BED

under my SPREAD.

Now, that ain't so bad huh?

Written by: Abiygayil C. Yisrael/

Rhymin Pearl

© 9 months ago,   rhyme • cozy • nature

Likes Rkorenfield

Rkorenfield - Thanks for your personal poem. I'm cold right now. It is chilly in FL. Enjoyed it

Rhymin Pearl - U welcome and thanks for the reading.

9 781729 585559